ystrica oravský podzámok zu

ská k

bojnice čičmany kremnica banská štiavnica banska

ejov košice bratislava trnava nitra piešťany trenčí

odzámok zuberec levoča spišská kapitula prešov b

kremnica banská štiavnica banská bystrica oravský

ava trnava nitra piešťany trenčín bojnice čičmany

levoča spišská kapitula prešov bardejov košice bra

štiavnica banská bystrica oravský podzámok zuber

piešťany trenčín bojnice čičmany kremnica banská

ula prešov bardejov košice bratislava trnava nitra

ca oravský podzámok zuberec levoča spišská kapit

čičmany kremnica banská štiavnica banská bystric

ce bratislava trnava nitra piešťany trenčín bojnice

zuberec levoča spišská kapitula prešov bardejov

SLOVAKIA

SLOVAKIA

alexandra nowack

slovart

The Slovak Republic has a rich cultural and architectural heritage. You will find more than a hundred castles and twice as many manor-houses, built during different historical epochs and having undergone a number of reconstructions. Some castles and fortresses were transformed during the 16th and 17th centuries into more comfortable and stylish units, which were inhabited by their owners up to the 20th century. The manor-houses, which replaced the medieval castles were mostly built on the flat land where small Gothic castles had stood. Their original function was defence, but from the end of the 16th century, comfort and style became more important. Slovakia has many well-preserved manor-houses from different architectural periods.

The building of churches and other religious buildings used for public Christian divine services came late in comparison with southern Europe. The first churches were not built until the 9th century during the time of the Great Moravian Empire. The architecture of the churches evolved for a thousand years as did the interiors, which were decorated in the spiritual traditions of each historical period. The simple and modest Romanesque decorations were gradually replaced by Gothic forms and architectural details. These were later enriched by Renaissance details e.g. paintings or sgraffiti. The Baroque style brought in splendidly designed interiors with wall painting, altar painting, plastic art and artisanal objects. Rococo, Classicism and the fashions of other ideals and periods only served to enhance the interiors of Slovak churches, many of which excel in their rich and varied decoration.

The wooden churches form a specific example of sacred architecture. The folk builders expressed in the house of God the harmony between the human spirit and nature and tried to gain a release from everyday life. The Gothic wooden churches are the oldest. Another type of church is the artikular church, built on the basis of a legal document (known as the Artikula) from the Emperor Leopold I. at the end of the 17th century. The ideas of the Reformation spread to the Kingdom of Hungary also, and the Emperor's decision permitted the building of two evangelical churches in some Hungarian regions. The Artikular churches, with the ground plan of a Greek cross, had to be built on the outskirts of the town, away from the city borders. They were not allowed to have a bell-tower, and the entrance had to be on the side facing away from the town.

cultural-history landmarks
and architecture

Bratislava (population: 429,000) is the capital city of the Slovak Republic, situated in the south-western part of the country. Bratislava stretches along both banks of the river Danube and to the foot of the Little Carpathian Mountains. The Danube is Europe's second longest river and it is Bratislava's glory. This strategically vital location several times played an important role in the history of Central Europe. In 1291 Bratislava was granted a municipal charter and became a free royal city. The 14th and 15th centuries were the golden age for Bratislava's trades and businesses. After the founding of the Istropolitana University (1467), Bratislava's influence strengthened as a centre of culture and knowledge in the Hungarian kingdom. When the Turkish armies penetrated deeper into the kingdom, Bratislava was, in 1536, declared the capital city of the Kingdom of Hungary, the seat of the congress, the central authority and the coronation city. Eleven kings and eight queens were crowned in Bratislava from 1563 to 1830. The war against the Turks and the civil insurrection had a negative influence on the city's economic development in the 16th and 17th centuries. In the 18th century, especially under the reign of Maria Teresa, Bratislava's importance

bratislava

grew once more. Many of the city's beautiful palaces and buildings date from this century. In the 19th century, the city became important as the centre of enlightenment and it was the birthplace of the Slovak National Uprising. Since 1918 it has been the political, business and cultural centre for all Slovaks. Now it is a modern contemporary city and the seat of political, government, business, social and scientific institutions. The city's symbol is the castle and the symbol of Christianity is St. Martin's Cathedral. One of the town's highlights is its wonderful tower with a replica of the royal crown of the Kingdom of Hungary, which serves as a reminder of the glory of the coronation days.

trnava

The pearl of Slovak cities is Trnava (population: 70,000), located in western Slovakia and also known as the "little Slovak Rome", because of its architectural and religious landmarks. The town was probably founded in the late 9th century at a crossroads of trade-routes as a small market town. At that time it was called Sobota (Saturday). The first reliable written reference to Trnava is from the year 1211, but more important is the document of privileges from King Bela IV dated 1238. This charter granted Trnava, as the first Slovak town to be so honoured, the status of free royal city. The greatest expansion was in the 16th century, when the city prospered and attracted new inhabitants. When Esztergom was occupied by the Turks in 1543, the archbishop of Esztergom and his canons moved to Trnava. The city then became the cultural and religious centre of the Hungarian Kingdom for nearly 300 years. A red-letter date was the year 1635 when Cardinal Peter Pazmany founded the university. Initially it only had the philosophy and theology faculties but these were afterwards augmented by the faculties of law and medicine. The 19th century also saw a revival of business in Trnava. The number of citizens increased and first and foremost the agricultural companies prospered. In 1846 the horse railway between Bratislava and Trnava was completed. Later on this was converted to a steam railway. Between the First and Second World Wars, Trnava was the third biggest town in Slovakia and became an important business and cultural centre in the western part of the country with a strong agricultural background. The city has maintained its position up to the present. It is the seat of the Trnava University and the St. Cyril and Method University and, since 1978, the metropolitan residence of the archbishop. In 1987 the city centre was declared a historical conservation area.

The biggest city in western Slovakia and the country's fourth biggest city is Nitra (population: 87, 000). In the records it is mentioned as the oldest settlement in Slovakia (source from the 70's of the 9th century). At the turn of the 9th century, an independent Nitran principality was established. It was headed by Earl Pribina, the first known monarch of the Slavs, probably the predecessors of Slovaks. Pribina built the first Christian church in Slovakia in 828 and Nitra became a part of the growing Great Moravian Empire. The 9th century saw the start of the history of the Nitra bishopric and the first monastery in Slovakia was established at this time. It survived the two following centuries and

nitra

later became a part of the Kingdom of Hungary. About the year 1000, the Esztergom archdiocese was founded with Nitra a diocese within it. In the archive of the Nitran diocese, two very precious parchments called Zoborské listiny (documents) are preserved. They date from the years 1111 and 1113 and are the oldest known original documents from the area of present-day Slovakia. In 1248 Nitra was granted the status of free royal city by king Belo IV. This related only to the lower part of the town and the castle, the rest remained under the aegis of the bishop. The bishops mostly respected the privileges of the citizens of Nitra, because this provided a guarantee for successful trade.

The subsequent development of the city was influenced by the wars in the 15th to 17th centuries. The final destructive incident in the town's history was the Rakoczi rising at the beginning of the 18th century. After the suppression of this revolt, the entire city had to be rebuilt. The rebuilding was in the Baroque style and enriched the city with several architectural landmarks. These are the pride of Nitra to this day. The beginning of the 19th century brought in the epoch of empiricism and classicism which gave the city its current appearance. In 1981 Nitra was declared a heritage conservation area.

The most famous spa in Slovakia is Piešťany (population: 31,000) located on a spur of Považský Inovec in western Slovakia. It is the most popular spa resort for the treatment of motor disorders. The presence of hot mineral springs with temperatures from 67°C to 69°C and sulphuric mud led to the expansion of bathing activity and the building of spa houses. The local mud has an extraordinary curative effect on inflammatory disorders and it is unique not just in Europe, but probably in the whole world. The first really significant owners were the Erdödy family, who built the first spa house in 1822 following the Napoleonic war, now known as the Old or Napoleon Spa. Real expansion and world renown came with the Winter family. At the beginning of the 20th century, several Art Nouveau hotels, such as Hotel Royal, Thermia Palace, Pro Patria and Excelsior (today Jalta), were built. In the 60's and 80's new spa houses were added and these days Piešťany has available 2, 400 beds in the middle and upper categories. These hotels stretched over an area of 40 hectares mainly in the city centre and the spa island, created by the river Váh and its branch. The spa park is a "city within a city"; with its sculptures and fountains it forms a most interesting venue. The park features a thermal swimming pool, a chain of sanatoria, health-curative facilities and hot springs. The spa's history is evoked by the well-preserved parts of the Gothic church and monastery of St. John, the Classical St. Stephen's Church and the Old (Napoleon) Spa building. The story of the spa's development in Piešťany is well explained in the Balneological Museum, located in a huge hall known as the Kursalon. Piešťany became well-known for its symbol – a sculpture of a man breaking his crutch. You can find it at the entrance to the Colonnade Bridge.

piešťany

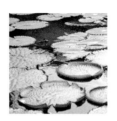

trenčín

Trenčín (population: 58,000) was for a long period the most important city in Slovakia, mainly due to its strategic location in the valley of the river Váh. When the Romans extended their borders to the Danube and set up the system of border forts known as the Limes Romanus, they started building fortified camps north of the Danube. The legions left behind them authentic proof of their presence in Trenčín. The Roman military settlement Laugaricio is the northern-most evidence of Roman expansion under the emperor Marcus Aurelius in Central Europe. The inscription on the Trenčín castle rock was carved to commemorate the victory over the Germanic people in A.D. 179. The first written record of the settlement situated under a great castle on the crossroads of trade-routes dates from the year 1111. The golden age for Trenčín was the end of the 13th century, when Peter Čák came into possession of the castle although the most rapid development came in the era of his son Matúš Čák, who became the emperor of the whole country. Trenčín acquired various privileges in medieval times. King Zigismund of Luxembourg granted the town the status of free royal city in 1412. In medieval times the city suffered attacks by the Turks, numerous battles in the Hungarian uprising, fires and natural disasters. But it always regained its interesting and beautiful appearance. After 1989 the historic city was revitalised and most of the old landmarks were restored. Since 1987 the city centre has been a historical town reserve. The symbol of the town and the surrounding county is the Trenčín castle built on a crag. The castle surrounds, a part of the Trenčín Museum, is formed by a collection of palaces and the evocative Matúš steeple.

One of the popular spa-resorts in central-western Slovakia is Bojnice spa (population: 5, 000). The history of this town is associated with the sulphuric thermal springs, known since medieval times. It was the Pálffy family that was credited with the greatest development of their use for curative purposes. The hot medicinal springs, ideal climate and one of the oldest and most beautiful spa parks in Slovakia provide the ideal environment for the treatment of motor and nervous system disorders. The spa mostly uses hydro-carbonic-calcium thermal water with a temperature of from 28°C to 52°C. The town's jewel is the "fairy tale" castle, one of the most visited and delightful heritage sites in

bojnice

Slovakia. It is built on a travertine mound, where a medieval castle stood in the 11th century. In the past, it was owned by the nobility, of whom the last owner was the Pálffy family. At the end of the 19th century, Earl Ján Pálffy rebuilt the whole castle in imitation of the style of the chateaux on the Loire in central France. The typical romantic outline of a medieval castle is created by its steep roofs, chapels and towers. Today there is an all-year-round exhibition of art-history. The greatest and most valuable exhibition piece is the late Gothic collection of paintings; the so-called Bojnice altar was made by the Florentine painter N. di Cione Ortagno in the mid-14th century.

The details of folk architecture and craftsmanship can be seen in a number of actual villages. Besides these, there are several skansens in Slovakia, which, together with the local culture and characteristic features, have become popular tourist attractions. Čičmany (population: 400), located in the north-western part of the country, is one of the most visited reserves. The first recorded reference to this municipality dates from 1272 when the locals were mostly farmers and shepherds. They were also skilled tradesmen and became famous for their embroidery and their folk costumes. Every visitor will be impressed by the unique decor on the wooden houses with the distinctive white ornamental painting composed from different geo-

čičmany

metrical shapes. The heritage site consists of 140 folk wooden houses. The ornamental painting on the side walls was supposed to protect the wooden beams from moisture and from cracks caused by the sun. At first, only the edges, the doors and window frames were painted white; subsequently, the white ornamentation appeared over the whole wooden surface. Women did the painting using clay and lime. The best preserved houses are the single-storey Raden's house and his neighbour Gregor's house, which houses an ethnographic exhibition.

The central Slovak town of Kremnica (population: 6,000) was one of the richest towns in the Hungarian kingdom. Its fame and riches were derived from gold mining, so it was also called the "golden town". The gold-bearing rocks in the local stream and the vein of gold ore were the reasons for the original settlement of Cremnychbana. In 1328 the Hungarian ruler Karl Robert conferred on it the privilege of a free royal and mining town. An essential privilege was the right to strike coins. The Kremnica Mint was established by mint workers who came from the Czech town of Kutná Hora at the invitation of the King. In 1329, only a year after it was built, the first Hungarian coins were struck. Besides these coins were also struck Kremnica ducats, which because of their quality and beauty, became one of the most popular currencies in Europe. In the 16th century the striking of medals was developed. To this day, commemorative coins and currencies of different countries are struck here. In 1405, the city built its outer fortification with walls, bastions and three gates. The trading privileges from King Matthew

kremnica

Korvin in 1474 helped the further rise of the town. However, the 16th century brought about a number of negative events. This was the century of Turkish attacks, epidemics and fire and finally the civil insurrection. Even in the 18th century the town's decline continued, although in spite of all, new Baroque buildings were built, which today form part of the town's conservation area. Kremnica's main symbol is the castle with a Gothic church from the 15th century. The church steeple on the piazza is open to the public and gives a wonderful view of the city and its surroundings. The pride of the church is its precious organ.

Without doubt, Banská Štiavnica (population 11,000) is one of the jewels of Slovakia. Situated in the Štiavnické vrchy (hills) in Central Slovakia, its undoubted quality and beauty secured the town its status as the first Slovak city to be listed as a UNESCO World Nature and Culture heritage site, in 1993. For a very long time, the city gained its prosperity from the mining of different ores, the most significant of which was silver, hence Banská Štiavnica was also known as the "silver city". The town was granted its first charter in 1238 and this charter was used as an example in the founding deeds for other central Slovak mining towns. The wealth derived from the ores was spent on constructing a glorious medieval town with the noble houses of rich bourgeois citizens (a.k.a. waldbürger), churches and public buildings. In the 18th century, Banská Štiavnica became the biggest centre for the output of precious metals in the Habsburg monarchy. Later, mining education and science were concentrated here. In 1735 the oldest mining school in the Hungarian kingdom was founded and in 1762 this was elevated to the status of Mining Academy – the first university of its kind in Europe. Fame and prosperity returned to the town at the end of the 18th century and Banská Štiavnica became the third biggest city in the Hungarian kingdom with 23,000 citizens. The end of the 19th century meant the decline of mining activities and this trend continued in the 20th century. The last mine in the Štiavnické hills closed in 2001. Today Banská Štiavnica is on the mend once more, this time as the centre for environmental research and education in Slovakia. There are 360 historical landmarks in Banská Štiavnica, where the main attraction is the Old Castle, the New Castle, churches and the Calvary.

banská štiavnica

banská bystrica

Banská Bystrica (population: 83,000) is the metropolis of Central Slovakia. It developed from a Slavic settlement, called Bystricia, and the number of inhabitants was increased by colonists from Germany. The main income was from mining. Banská Bystrica, also called the "copper city", was one of the three richest mining towns in central Slovakia. In the 15th century, the German banker and tradesman Jakub Fugger and count Ján Thurzo started a business

together. When their kin intermarried, the Thurzo-Fugger trading company was established and soon it had almost a monopoly position over the world copper market. In the 16th century the metal market began to stagnate due to competition from abroad and the negative impact on the town of the Turkish attacks. The castle was rebuilt as a modern anti-Turkish fortress that repulsed the Turkish army. The structure of Banská Bystrica's economy changed in the 18th century. The process-

ing of iron ore took over from copper mining. Intense demands were made on the surrounding forests. Following the great fire in 1761, the city took on a new appearance in a largely Baroque-style. In the middle of the 20th century, Banská Bystrica featured significantly upon the world's stage as, in 1944, it was the birthplace and centre of the Slovak National Uprising. The greatest nation-wide revolt against Nazism during the course of World War II took place here.

Another attraction is the north Slovak town of Oravský Podzámok (population: 1,500) situated near the Polish border. It is located on the river Orava under a majestic rock cliff. In the past, the settlement led a busy trading and social life with some artisans' companies working here but the business importance of the town declined in the 20th century. Like many other castles in Slovakia, this was probably built on the foundations of a former wooden castle ruined after the Tatar invasion in 1241. In 1370 it became the country castle and the seat of power for the owner of almost the whole Orava region. The castle on the rock was originally built in the Romanesque and Baroque styles, then later rebuilt with a Renaissance and Neo-Gothic appearance. It is constructed as a set of buildings which follow the shape of the castle rock. In 1556 it came into the ownership of the Thurzo family, which carried out many modifications. Today's appearance has changed little since 1611. After the Thurzo family died out, the castle was owned by various other families who neglected it. The greatest catastrophe was the fire in 1800; after that it was no longer of any use to its owners. Extensive reconstruction work to save the castle was carried out after the end of World War II. Today it comprises a magnificent set of lower, middle and upper keeps with palaces, fortifications and towers. A major attraction is the three gates connected by a tunnel and casemates.

oravský podzámok

A special characteristic of the Orava region is its wooden folk architecture, which you can find in Zuberec (population: 2,000) and the surrounding area. Not far from here, on the Brestová plateau, is a special model village – the Museum of Orava Villages. It is located in the midst of the beautiful countryside of the Western Tatras. Through the middle of the village flows the Studený potok (Cold Stream), and on its banks stands a 20 hectare village made up from the characteristic folk buildings from each of the Orava regions. Visitors can see residential as well as farm buildings (residential houses, farms, store-rooms, hay-lofts, a chalet etc.) sacred buildings (a wooden church, a cemetery, bell to-wers) and Orava artisans' buildings (craftsman's workshop, shepherd's building and saw mill, fuller's workshop, forge, pottery kiln etc.). The museum is divided into five different architectural parts. The Dolnooravský rínok represents the wealthy region of lower Orava with exquisite buildings and extends over the greatest part. Mlynica by the stream focuses on the water mill, saw mill and fulling shed used for cloth working with its water driven machinery. Zamagurská ulica (street), with the houses and farm buildings of the rich and middle class farmers, displays the characteristic structure of an Orava village. Goralské lazy represents the poor areas of the Orava region situated on the south-eastern slopes of the Oravské Beskydy. Poor woodcutter/shepherd's and farmer's houses with an earth floor and an open fireplace can be seen here. The dominant feature is the church-yard and late-Gothic wooden church of St. Elisabeth from Zábrežie from the 15th century, standing on a raised site.

zuberec

Spiš is a historical region of northern Slovakia which contains a number of cultural and architectural sites. Probably the most popular town in this area is Levoča (population: 14, 000), first mentioned in a document dated 1249 under the name Leucha. This settlement, located on the strategic trade route known as the Via Magna (Great Route) very soon grew into a town with several privileges. In a short period of time Levoča became the centre of German colonization in the Spiš region and in 1271 it was elevated as the capital city of the Spiš-Saxon community. Subsequent developments resulted in a reduction of the power of the community, which led eventually to the declaration of Levoča as a free royal city in 1323. The privilege to store goods imported from Poland, Silesia, Germany and Russia helped to boost the economy. Trade was the driving force in Levoča, and it took on an international dimension. The tradesmen in Levoča produced goods not only for the local markets but for markets and fairs over the whole of the Hungarian kingdom and Poland. Later the town became one of the main centres for the Renaissance and Humanism in the Hungarian kingdom. Levoča is constructed as a group of culturally important buildings surrounded by relatively well-preserved town walls. In old Levoča, the star attraction is the rectangular Central Square, with two churches and the Town Hall situated in the middle. The most renowned is the church of St. Jakub with a late-Gothic main altar, 18.6 metres high. It is the highest altar of its kind in the world, and it was made from lime wood at the beginning of the 16th century in the workshop of Master Paul of Levoča. Next to the parish church is the seat of the former Town Hall of Levoča with arcades built after the fire in 1550. It is one of the most precious non-sacred-Renaissance buildings in Slovakia. The central square is surrounded by more than fifty bourgeois and patrician's houses of note.

levoča

HIN GEHET DIE ZEIT
HER KOMPT DER TODT
O MENSCH THUE BUES
VND FÜRCHTE GOT

spišská kapitula

The heart of the Spiš region has always been the Spiš Castle which, with an area of more than four hectares, is the most extensive castle ruin in Central Europe. The region was controlled both by the clergy and the castle. The religious life in Spiš was organized by the Provost, bishops and monks from Spišská Kapitula. In the valley between these two centres of power developed the town of Spišské Podhradie (population: 3,500) a part of which is the heritage conservation area of Spišská Kapitula. It has held the status of church town since the 12th century. The religious environment prompts visitors to compare the town under Spiš Castle with the Vatican. The Kapitula priory began its activities in 1198 and soon after a canonry was added. In the 13th century the building of the cathedral and priory palace was begun. The town walls with two gates were built in the 14th century and reconstructed several times. Its present-day appearance with two late-Renaissance gates dates from the second half of the 17th century, when the Hungarian kingdom was threatened by the Osman Empire. Fortunately, the Spiš region was spared from Turkish occupation and major attacks. The Kapitula Provosts tried to promote the priory into a bishopric; this was repeatedly refused by the Archbishop in Esztergom. Finally, it attained the status of bishopric in 1776 and holds it to this day. The most famous building in the town is the late-Gothic St. Martin's Cathedral. In 1382 the Corpus Christi chapel was added, which was later replaced by the current Zápoľský chapel built in imitation of the French Sainte Chapelle. The Episcopal Palace was built at the same time as the cathedral. From 1281 it underwent several Renaissance and Baroque reconstructions.

The metropolis of Šariš, the north-eastern region of Slovakia, is Prešov (population: 93,000), the third largest city in Slovakia. For many hundreds of years the town competed with Košice and Bardejov in the struggle for the traditional dominant position in eastern Slovakia. After it was granted the king's charter in 1370, the town became a free royal town and in 1480 a member of the Pentapolitana (a group of five east-Slovak towns). The Reformation started well in the 16th and 17th centuries and Prešov became an important bastion for reformation churches in the Hungarian kingdom. Besides positive developments in trade and business, education and culture also flourished. In the town was an Evangelical College that provided a good education following the tenets of the Reformation and Humanism. This was delivered by teachers who came here as fresh graduates from German universities. Thanks to them, Prešov was also called the "Athens by the Torysa" and in 1647 became the county town of the Šariš County. After a short economic stagnation at the beginning of the 18th century, activity was revitalised and the city returned to its role as the centre of the region. The city's landmarks are concentrated in the historical city centre spread around the Main Street, which widens into a rectangular square. The most note-worthy sights are in the middle. The dominant landmark is the 14th century Church of St. Nicholas with its high steeple. This triple-naved Gothic cathedral was completed in 1515.

presov

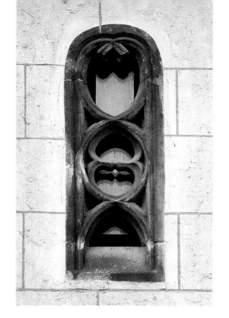

bardejov

The ancient town of Bardejov (population: 33,000) is located in north-eastern Slovakia and is without doubt one of the most beautiful towns in Slovakia. In 1986 it was deservedly awarded the prestigious European medal – gold medal by the UNESCO ICOMOS foundation and in 2001 Bardejov was included as a listed site in the UNESCO World Heritage list. The city's development was helped by some royal privileges but mainly by its declaration as a free royal town by King Ludovít I in 1376. Bardejov's golden age was in the 15th century during which, with its economic success driven by business and trade, it became one of the most influential cities in the Hungarian kingdom. In the 16th century the city was at the fore-front of new ideas in culture and education. The bearers were mostly Renaissance and Reformation-Humanism representatives coming in the main from Germany. A less successful era in Bardejov's history was the 17th century, noted for a series of civil insurrections. The town was overshadowed by the more successful Prešov. It is claimed that Bardejov is the most Gothic city in Slovakia. The city centre is a full set of prized historic buildings arranged in a pear-shaped ground plan, and surrounded by an almost unbroken ring of city fortifications.

The most noteworthy part of the historical centre is the rectangular square surrounded by old townhouses with typical gable fronts with Rococo frescoes. In the middle of the square stands the house of the former Town Hall from the 16th century, an example of the combination of Renaissance and the early transalpine Renaissance architecture. Occupying the most imposing site in the square is the 15th century parish church. It is a glorious Gothic basilica with three naves. Bardejov is also justifiably proud of its town walls, which are the best preserved medieval defensive system in Slovakia.

The Eastern Slovak metropolis and Slovakia's second biggest city is Košice (population: 236, 000). It is located on the river Hornád and for hundreds of years it has been the most important location in the region, a centre for business, trade, culture and education. The history of this medieval town stretches back to the year 1230. German settlers settled here in a region devastated by the Tatars in 1241 and 1242. After their arrival in the second half of the 13th century, the era of successful development followed. Citizens of German origin forged a chain of active business connections over the whole of Europe and in 1342 the town was awarded its charter as a free royal town. A most important date for Košice was the year 1369 when it became the first European town to receive a coat of arms document signed by the King. The town enjoyed great success up to the middle of the 15th century and it became, after Buda, the second biggest town in the Hungarian kingdom. Later development was slowed not only by the Turkish wars but also by insurrections. Under their influence, business and trade began to decline and the number of citizens reduced. The 18th century passed by calmly and then, in the second half of the 19th century, the town walls were pulled down and new residential and industrial quarters were built. You don't have to walk very far to see Košice's landmarks; almost all of them are situated in the historical city centre, which is the biggest historical town conservation area in Slovakia. The central area is an elongated square, which is rightly considered one of the most beautiful of Slovak squares. The most prized individual buildings are located in the middle and the dominant building, not only in the square but in the whole city, is the Gothic St. Elisabeth's Cathedral, which is the biggest church in Slovakia and Europe's eastern-most cathedral built in the western style.

košice

other sights

trenčín

Trenčín Castle, Church of the Virgin Mary's Birth, Town Gate, the Church and Monastery of St. Francis Xavier, M. A. Bazovský Gallery, County House, the Trenčín Museum, Church of Notre Dame

bratislava

Bratislava castle, St. Martin's Cathedral, Gerulata, Devín Castle, St. Michael's Tower, Mirbach's Palace, Pálffy's Palace, Presidential Palace, Primate's Palace, the Slovak National Theatre, the Old Town Hall

bojnice

Bojnice Castle, Zoo, Spa, International Ghosts and Monsters Festival, St. Martin's Church

trnava

St. Nicholas Parish Church, St. John the Baptist Cathedral, St. Jacob's Church, the Town Tower, Ján Palárik Theatre, Trinity Church, the Town Hall, the Museum of Western Slovakia

čičmany

Raden's house, Gregor's house

nitra

St. Emeran's Church, Nitra Castle, St. Michael's Church, the Great Seminar, Kluch Palace, the Franciscan Church and Monastery, the County House, Piarists' Church and Monastery

kremnica

Town Castle, the Franciscan Church and Monastery, Mint, Coins and Medals Museum, Lower Gate

piešťany

the Spa, Church and Monastery, St. Stephen's Church, Napoleonic Spa, Balneological Museum, Colonnade Bridge

levoča

St. Jacob's Church, the Town Hall, the Bell Tower, Waaghause Building, County House, Thurzo's House, Mariasy's House, Minorities' Monastery, the Church of the Holy Spirit.

banská štiavnica

the Old Castle, the Mining Museum in nature, the New Castle, Virgin Mary's Church, Piarská Gate, St. Catherine's Church, Chamber Court, Calvary

spišská kapitula

the Bishop's Palace, the Clock Tower, Zápoľský Chapel, St. Martin's Cathedral

banská bystrica

City Castle, the Clock Tower, St. Francis Xavier's Church, Thurzo's house, Beniczky's house, Bishop's Palace, St. Elizabeth's Church, the Nation House

prešov

Evangelical College, Klobučický Palace, Rákóczi Palace, St. John the Baptist's Cathedral, Caraff's House, the complex of the Franciscan Church and Monastery

oravský podzámok

Castle of Orava

bardejov

St. Egidius's Church, Bardejov Spa, the Museum of Folk Architecture, the Town Hall, the Šariš Museum, Gantzunhof, St. John the Baptist's Church and Monastery

zuberec

the Museum of Orava Villages, Podroháč Folk Festival

košice

St. Elizabeth's Cathedral, Urban's Tower, St. Michael's Chapel, Church and Monastery, Rákóczi Palace, Executioner's Bastion, Mikluš Prison, Dominican Church, St. Nicholas's Church

Alexandra Nowack, also called Sasha, was born in 1973 as German in the Slovak town of Nitra. In 1995 she went to Sydney (Australia) for one year in order to study photography. In 1997 Sasha began to study at the Academy of Art in Bratislava being tutored by the well known academic architect J. Krížik. In 1998 she transferred to Dortmund (Germany) to study photo design with Prof. H. Schmitz.

This book is Alexandra Nowack's 2003 graduation portfolio. Since then she has worked as a freelance photographic designer. In her pictures Sasha tries to concentrate not only on the entire image, but rather on enhancing the detail. She tries therefore to direct the onlooker to these details and the full final image is created from the mesh of smaller images.

bojnice čičmany kremnica banská štiavnica bansk

ardejov košice bratislava trnava nitra piešťany tren

podzámok zuberec levoča spišská kapitula prešov b

y kremnica banská štiavnica banská bystrica oravs

tislava trnava nitra piešťany trenčín bojnice čičma

levoča spišská kapitula prešov bardejov košice bra

štiavnica banská bystrica oravský podzámok zube

itra piešťany trenčín bojnice čičmany kremnica bar

apitula prešov bardejov košice bratislava trnava n

ystrica oravský podzámok zuberec levoča spišská

ojnice čičmany kremnica banská štiavnica banská b

košice bratislava trnava nitra piešťany trenčín boj

k zuberec levoča spišská kapitula prešov bardejov

nica banská štiavnica banská bystrica oravský podz